BLACK
CROSSWORD

BLACK CROSSWORD

100 Mini Puzzles
CELEBRATING
THE African Diaspora

JULIANA PACHE

AMISTAD

An Imprint of HarperCollinsPublishers

HarperCollins books may be purchased for educational, business, or sales promotional use. For information, please email the Special Markets Department at SPsales@harpercollins.com.

FIRST EDITION

Designed by Nancy Singer

Library of Congress Cataloging-in-Publication Data has been applied for.

ISBN 978-0-06-339029-4

24 25 26 27 28 LBC 5 4 3 2 1

For all of us connected
For all of us rooted
For all of us proud

When I need to say words that do more than simply mirror or address the dominant reality, I speak black vernacular. There, in that location, we make English do what we want it to do. We take the oppressor's language and turn it against itself. We make our words a counter-hegemonic speech, liberating ourselves in language.

——BELL HOOKS

I'm dark brown, dark skin, light skin, beige, fluorescent beige . . . I'm Black.

——TS MADISON

INTRODUCTION

I love starting my day with a stimulating challenge, followed by a sense of completion. One morning in October 2022, I did my morning routine of completing quick, fun digital word games when I was stumped by a crossword clue that, to be honest, felt very white. As in, "Hwhite." And while I didn't necessarily think that was some kind of injustice in that instance (one of the beautiful things about crosswords is the opportunity to learn new information and make connections), I wondered if a daily Black-culture-focused crossword puzzle existed online. After doing many searches, and not finding anything current or updated regularly, I decided to launch a daily puzzle myself, and thus, in January 2023, Black Crossword was born.

The world of crossword puzzles (also known as the "Crossworld") has historically been dominated by white male constructors. While the industry is slowly diversifying, people across various identities are actively pushing for inclusion in these spaces. While inclusion is important, Black Crossword aims to stand on its own, in celebration of our cultures, our dialects, and the figures we cherish.

While creating Black Crossword, I contemplated the ways our cultures intersect with one another across the globe, how they are connected, and how they cannot be siphoned off into separate pieces—kind of like the words in a crossword puzzle.

I was a casual crossword solver when I started this endeavor, but I've been passionate about researching Black culture and history since my teen years when I worked in my local library. Later, during my work-study at the Temple University library where I had access to a plethora of stimulating materials, I fell in love with learning more about the richness of the diaspora and developed a deeper understanding of myself and people who look like me. During the creation of these puzzles, I often pull on the knowledge I gathered during that time, as well as my lived experiences as a Black Caribbean American woman in community with other Black folks.

While researching and compiling terms for Black Crossword's word library, I often think about Arturo Alfonso Schomburg, a Harlem Renaissance historian whose life's work was documenting the accomplishments of Afro-descendants. His efforts were sparked by the desire to correct a schoolteacher in Puerto Rico who told him that Black people have no history. I'm familiar with this particular flavor of anti-blackness—that being, the insidious and pervasive whitewashing of history within the Spanish-speaking Caribbean, as both sides of my family immigrated to New York City from Cuba and the Dominican Republic between the '60s and '80s. Via subtle and sometimes blatant communication, I learned that several of my family members, while not necessarily in denial about their ancestry, did not value their African lineage—a mentality perhaps bred from a desire to elevate their social status, not uncommon across the diaspora. Nonetheless, I had an insatiable desire to affirm myself and my Blackness, in spite of these attempts to muddle my heritage, to do something about my *pelo malo* (bad hair), and to ignore that our customs are obviously rooted in African traditions. In this way, Schomburg's path to researching and celebrating the diaspora is one I deeply relate to.

Simultaneously, I cherish this perspective from Toni Morrison:

> The function, the very serious function of racism is distraction. It keeps you from doing your work. It keeps you explaining, over and over again, your reason for being. Somebody says you have no language and you spend twenty years proving that you do. Somebody says your head isn't shaped properly so you have scientists working on the fact that it is. Somebody says you have no art, so you dredge that up. Somebody says you have no kingdoms, so you dredge that up. None of this is necessary. There will always be one more thing.

My hunger for the constant affirmation provided by digging through Black historical texts in my local and college libraries blossomed into a calm and matter-of-fact knowing of Black culture's richness throughout my adulthood. I value Schomburg's methodology, as well as Morrison's, and aim to combine these principles into the ethos of Black Crossword. These puzzles are created with the aim to affirm and connect us, showcasing our terms and the ways we use them, while not owing anyone an explanation. While everyone is welcome and invited to solve and learn from these puzzles, they are *for* us, full stop.

My hope for you, the solver, is that you enjoy the puzzles included here (created with our connected cultures in mind), find stimulation in the mental challenge, and collect new information about your "cousins" across the globe.

Most of all, I hope you see yourself.

PUZZLES

1.

1	2	3		
4			5	6
7				
	8			
	9			

ACROSS

1 "A Change Is Gonna Come" singer Cooke

4 Also known as

7 Studio 54, for one

8 SZA's debut album title

9 Visually inspected

DOWN

1 Feeling blue

2 *The Color Purple* writer Walker

3 Ballerina Copeland

5 Land unit

6 Auction-ending word

2.

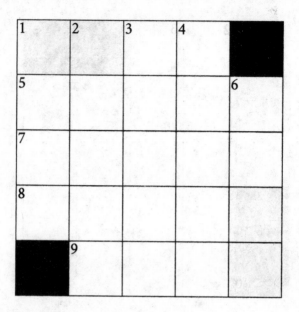

ACROSS

1 Season that follows summer

5 Give permission for

7 Put on, as a protest

8 "Stranger in My House" singer

9 Ribs unit

DOWN

1 Tracy Chapman's "___ Car"

2 Designated space for honoring spirits such as orishas

3 Alpaca relative

4 Sound reasoning

6 I'm ___ (slang for "that's hilarious")

3.

1	2	3		
4			5	6
7				
	8			
	9			

ACROSS

1 Black magazine founded in 1951, known for its iconic covers
4 "Sweet Love" singer Baker
7 Black girl ____
8 Camping shelter
9 Historic chapters

DOWN

1 *Space* ____
2 Related on the mother's side
3 Striped predator
5 "Private Dancer" singer Turner
6 Play divisions

4.

ACROSS

1 Future flower
4 Part of AAPI
7 Celia Cruz is known as the queen of this genre
8 Very smooth
9 "Old Town Road" rapper, Lil ___ X

DOWN

1 Esperanza Spalding's instrument
2 Jamaican sprinter Bolt
3 Detroit musician and record producer, J ___
5 Inquires
6 Politician's "no" vote

5.

¹	²	³		
⁴			⁵	⁶
⁷				
⁸				
	⁹			

ACROSS

1 CEO's degree, often

4 Come up

7 Kitchen flooring pieces

8 Fragrance

9 The Internet singer and producer, Syd Tha ____

DOWN

1 Yoga class needs

2 Marsha P. Johnson threw one at the 1969 Stonewall uprising

3 American Dance Theater founder Alvin

5 2000 D'Angelo song, "____ It On"

6 Approx.

6.

	1	2	3	4
5				
6				
7				
8				

ACROSS

1 Go ____ in the paint
5 Charity supporter
6 Not called for
7 Arranges by kind
8 Ancestry diagrams

DOWN

1 Pay tribute to
2 One half of Outkast, ____ 3000
3 Nat King Cole's "____ 66"
4 "Freakum" attire Beyoncé recommends you put on when your man acts wrong
5 1991 Julie Dash film, *Daughters of the* ____

7.

1	2	3	4	■
5				6
7				
8				
9				

ACROSS

1 Purchase price
5 Relating to the eye
7 Enticing smell
8 Stores for a rainy day
9 Jackson 5 hit, "I'll Be ___"

DOWN

1 Ivory ___
2 Media mogul Winfrey
3 Appliance with burners
4 Hourglass, e.g.
6 "Touch Me Tease Me" singer

8.

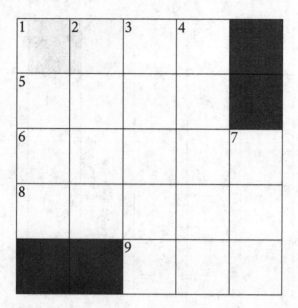

ACROSS

1 Pizza-crust choice

5 Flower with thorns

6 PR concern

8 June birthstone

9 2015 NFL MVP Newton

DOWN

1 Don't ___ (slang for "don't overreact")

2 A house is not one, according to Luther Vandross

3 "Shaft" composer Hayes

4 Joe Arroyo's 1988 classic about a slave uprising in Colombia, "La rebelión (No le pegue a la ___)"

7 Shady tree

9.

ACROSS

1 "What it do?"
4 "Buy U a Drank" singer
7 "All kidding ___ . . ."
8 Extend one's lease
9 "At Last" singer James

DOWN

1 Lingering look
2 None too pleased
3 Ice cream ___ job
5 Concept
6 "Can You Stand the Rain" group, ___ Edition

10.

	1	2	3	
4				5
6				
7				
8				

ACROSS

1 Spit rhymes
4 Got a new address
6 Lose strength
7 Warm-weather fabric
8 Contest submission

DOWN

1 ABC host Roberts
2 The "Black Godfather" of entertainment Clarence
3 Tosh of Bob Marley and the Wailers
4 One of the sexes
5 Opposite of admit

11.

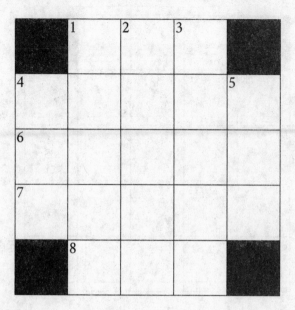

ACROSS

1 Txt

4 *Feminism Is for Everybody* author bell

6 Protagonist in Michael Jackson's "Smooth Criminal"

7 Sorority founded at Howard University in 1913,
  Delta ____ Theta

8 Purchase, in slang

DOWN

1 Video game hedgehog

2 "Watermelon Man" jazz musician Santamaria

3 Pinch pennies

4 The time ____ come

5 Caribbean or Caspian

12.

ACROSS

1 That's a ___ (rejection or failure, in slang)

4 Cockpit figure

6 Opening remarks

7 Shift-6 symbol

8 Throw ___ (subtly critique, in slang)

DOWN

1 "What a Difference a Day Makes" singer Washington

2 Debut mixtape by Frank Ocean, *Nostalgia,* ___

3 Not at all interested

4 JPEGs or PNGs

5 Canvas bag

13.

ACROSS

1 Say grace, perhaps
5 Slick Rick the ___
7 Diva's performance
8 *Madea* director and producer Tyler
9 1996 film starring Jada Pinkett, Queen Latifah, Vivica A. Fox, and Kimberly Elise, ___ *It Off*

DOWN

1 Respect, in slang
2 Indian coin
3 Emergency notification
4 A New Yorker's "hello"
6 Charles who played piano

19

14.

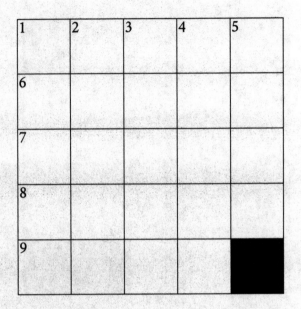

ACROSS

1 Take as one's own
6 *Shake Loose My Skin* author Sanchez
7 Look of contempt
8 Make into law
9 Tall story

DOWN

1 Valuable holding
2 Disco diva Summer
3 Lakers legend Shaquille
4 Fragment
5 Like cranberries

15.

	1	2	3	4
5				
6				
7				
8				

ACROSS

1 Toni Cade Bambara novel, *The* ____ *Eaters*

5 Debut album by Travis Scott

6 Homo sapiens

7 Martini garnish

8 Fall blossom

DOWN

1 Sociology studies staple by W. E. B. Du Bois, *The* ____ *of Black Folk*

2 Fess up

3 Head for the door

4 Skin care or printer product

5 Reality show with Georgia peaches, Abbr.

16.

ACROSS

1 Boo-hoo

5 The "Godfather of Vogue," ____ Ninja

6 Still kicking

7 Try to prevent

8 Zora Neale Hurston's *Their* ____ *Were Watching God*

DOWN

1 Painter of Barack Obama's portrait for the National Portrait Gallery, Kehinde ____

2 Cream of the crop

3 North Pole workers

4 Place to dock

5 "____ in the Water"

17.

ACROSS

1 Doorstep item
4 Gospel singer Yolanda
7 Tiny hairs
8 Archnemesis
9 Desert refuge

DOWN

1 Afro-Cuban abolitionist and general, Antonio ____
2 "Freak Like Me" singer Howard
3 2021 Jazmine Sullivan album, *Heaux* ____
5 Mariah Carey's *The Emancipation of* ____
6 Articulates

18.

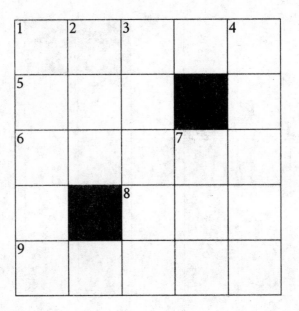

ACROSS

1 Burst of light

5 Title for Raphael Warnock, for short

6 10 ____ or less lane

8 Rebellion leader Turner

9 DJ's collection

DOWN

1 Prepared catfish or chicken

2 Frankie Beverly and Maze classic, "Before I ____ Go"

3 Arctic bloom

4 Party throwers

7 Baked ____ and cheese

19.

ACROSS

1 CD-___

4 Music of Trinidad's carnival

5 Injures

6 Inventive thoughts

7 Fashion legend, André ___ Talley

DOWN

1 Aventura lead singer Santos

2 Most of the earth

3 Easter service

4 "Kiss of Life" singer

5 Mama or Wayne

20.

1	**2**	**3**	**4**	■
5				**6**
7				
8				
■	**9**			

ACROSS

1 "I just want your extra time and your ___" (Prince lyric)

5 One doing nothing

7 Exchange

8 Largest moon of Saturn

9 Email status

DOWN

1 Catwoman actress Eartha

2 Damson of *Snowfall*

3 Roofing tile

4 Four-door car

6 Landlord's collection

21.

ACROSS

1 Quick punch

4 Baby-faced

5 "___ funk," a.k.a. Brazilian funk

6 Best actress award for Halle Berry, making her the first Black woman to win

7 Picks up the tab

DOWN

1 Rags-to-riches anthem by The Notorious B.I.G.

2 Book of maps

3 Draft beverage

4 "Mi ___ es tu ___"

5 Catchy song

27

22.

1		2	3	4
5	6			
7				
8				
9				

ACROSS

2 Cul-de-____

5 Regular's order, with "the"

7 Time off

8 Thrifty one

9 "She ____ that!" (She did an exceptional job.)

DOWN

1 "Black Wall Street" city

2 Debonair

3 Black language letters

4 Judge's aide

6 Shirley Chisholm quote, "If they don't give you a ____ at the table, bring a folding chair."

23.

1	2	3	4	
5				
6				7
8				
9				

ACROSS

1 Chance of a loss
5 2016 Rihanna album
6 Take the wheel
8 Playfully taunt
9 Packing heat

DOWN

1 Afrocentric believer in Jah
2 Prefix with stellar or galactic
3 Vapor from a sauna
4 *Heavy* author Laymon
7 Color on the Pan-African flag

24.

1	2	3		
4			5	6
7				
8				
9				

ACROSS

1 Government med-approving body, Abbr.

4 "It Ain't Over 'Til It's Over" singer Kravitz

7 Aquarium accumulation

8 ____ on (overlooked, in slang)

9 Green smoothie ingredient

DOWN

1 Liquor canteen

2 "Don't You Know?" singer Reese

3 1998 hit from Monica, "____ of Mine"

5 Neck part

6 To date

25.

	1	2	3	4
5				
6				
7				■
8				■

ACROSS

1 Minor quarrel
5 Sweet, in Italy
6 No longer sleeping
7 Caribbean carnival party
8 Chart with ancestors

DOWN

1 Octavia E. Butler novel, *Parable of the* ____
2 Make yourself one at a cookout
3 National fruit of Jamaica
4 Yup, in my white ____
5 Obtuse

31

26.

ACROSS

1 Astrological border

5 African language family

6 Belted constellation

7 Intense suffering

8 R&B group Tony! Toni! ____!

DOWN

1 Popular pants type

2 Gabrielle of *Being Mary Jane*

3 1972 song by The Temptations, "Papa Was a Rollin' ____"

4 Small and weak

5 Gravy holder

27.

1	2	3		
4			5	6
7				
8				
9				

ACROSS

1 Comedian, Bernie ____

4 Traditional saying

7 Snooped

8 West African storyteller

9 Popular card game where house rules must be established

DOWN

1 Popular Dominican dish that originates from the Congo region of Africa

2 Embellish

3 Brand of keyboards and watches

5 Earth prefix

6 NYC summer hrs.

28.

ACROSS

1 Catch waves

5 Unoriginal

6 Become allied

7 Glove material

8 Places you might sit at the dock of

DOWN

1 *Brown Sugar* actress Lathan

2 Black feminist anthem by Queen Latifah

3 Freelancer's quotes

4 DJ and record producer, Funkmaster ___

5 Light in a lamp

29.

1	2	3		
4			5	
6				7
	8			
	9			

ACROSS

1 Lil ____, the Queen Bee

4 Rapper and *New Jack City* actor

6 ____ wave

8 Naughty's opposite

9 Fence entrance

DOWN

1 First-aid ____

2 Cupcake topper

3 Communications industry

5 Diplomatic skill

7 *Do the Right Thing* director Spike

30.

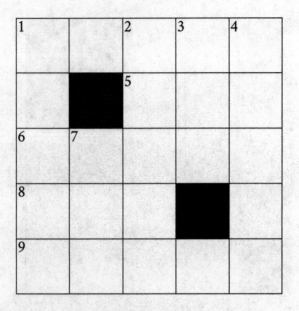

ACROSS

1 Philadelphia songstress Jill

5 Combat

6 Proof of innocence

8 Take the gold

9 Actress Ruth of *Passing*

DOWN

1 1997 Michael Jai White superhero film

2 Having debts

3 Bar bill

4 *Diamond Princess* rapper from Miami

7 Be untruthful

31.

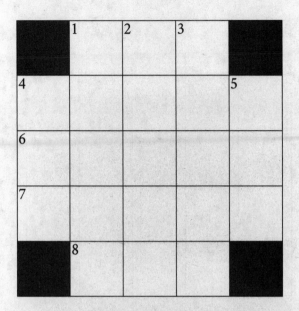

ACROSS

1 February observance for the legacies of African descendants, Abbr.

4 Standoffish

6 Rajon of the NBA

7 Old manuscript

8 Beaver's project

DOWN

1 1998 DMX album, *Flesh of My Flesh,* ____ *of My* ____

2 Civic automaker

3 Wi-Fi device

4 Rainbow's shape

5 Vivica A. or Rick

32.

1	2	3	4	5
6				
7				
8				
9				

ACROSS

1 Philadelphia rap crew led by Beanie Sigel, ____ Property
6 "She reminds me of a West Side Story"
7 Riley who played Mercedes Jones on *Glee*
8 Basketball or football
9 Abrasive

DOWN

1 Huge hit
2 City on Florida's Gulf Coast
3 Shady spot
4 Organizational levels
5 Venus neighbor

33.

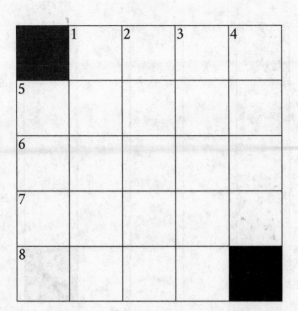

ACROSS

1 Southern subgenre of hip-hop

5 TV ad

6 Pink drinks

7 Offer one's two cents

8 2002 song from The Roots, "The ___ (2.0)"

DOWN

1 "Jezebel" or "Angry Black Woman," for example

2 Perez of *White Men Can't Jump*

3 Adjust, as tax returns

4 FX show starring Billy Porter and Michaela Jaé Rodriguez

5 ___ and cons

34.

1	2	3	4	5
6				
7				
8				
9				■

ACROSS

1 Hardwood tree
6 Birth city of Malcolm X
7 ____ Rights Act of 1964
8 Funeral sound
9 1979 song from Stevie Wonder, "____ One Your Love"

DOWN

1 Anti-theft devices
2 "Caroline" rapper from Portland
3 Actress ____-Symoné
4 Billie Holiday jazz standard "God Bless the ____"
5 *Girls Trip* actress Regina

35.

ACROSS

1 Montgomery ___ boycott

4 Exploit, as power

6 Headwear for a Black Panther Party member

7 Hits the tarmac

8 Geologic time unit

DOWN

1 *African Giant* musician, ___ Boy

2 John Legend's debut single, "___ to Love U"

3 Complete collections

4 Qualified

5 Honey lover

36.

1	2	3	4	5
6				
7				
8				
9				

ACROSS

1 Docket items

6 44

7 U or I, e.g.

8 Planner entry

9 "Love T.K.O." singer Pendergrass

DOWN

1 Yearn for

2 1994 sports drama starring Duane Martin and Tupac Shakur, ____ the Rim

3 Did some carpentry

4 Make corrections to

5 Annoyed or disappointed, in slang

37.

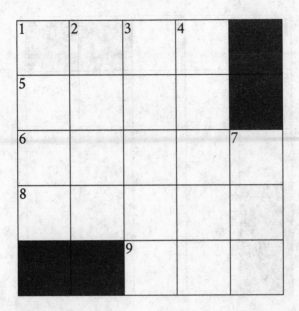

ACROSS

1 Tibia's place
5 Bonet or Lopes
6 Metal mixture
8 Culpability
9 South Florida city, for short

DOWN

1 Texas slang for a candy-painted car that rides low to the ground
2 *Black Feminist Thought* author, Patricia ____ Collins
3 Muhammad Ali's faith
4 Supermodel Campbell
7 Affirmative vote

38.

1	2	3		
4			5	6
7				
	8			
	9			

ACROSS

1 2015 NFL MVP Newton

4 Bring shame to

7 Dwarf planet beyond Neptune

8 Egg-shaped

9 Present!

DOWN

1 Untrue, in slang

2 Off-White fashion designer Virgil

3 Pale purple hue

5 Rose Royce ballad, "Wishing on a ___"

6 Center of a bagel

39.

	1	2	3	
4				5
6				
7				
8				

ACROSS

1 "Don't be a hard rock when you really are a ____" (Lauryn Hill lyric)

4 Team race

6 Model and actor Moore who starred as Angel in FX's *Pose*

7 1994 classic from Wu-Tang Clan

8 "Best Part" R&B singer

DOWN

1 Calypso, for example

2 Senior

3 "Phenomenal Woman" writer Angelou

4 Wealthy

5 Candied veggie

40.

ACROSS

1 Core muscles

4 Jollof

6 "Ring the ___, another sound is dying, woh-oh, hey" (Tenor Saw lyric)

8 Prove false

9 Religious branch

DOWN

1 The "A" of UAE

2 Most decorated gymnast Simone

3 On a ___ from 1 to 10

5 Comedian ___ André

7 Crossed paths

41.

ACROSS

1 "Thanks for coming to my ___ talk"

4 Ocean's rise or fall

5 Vocal extent

6 Strongly recommend

7 Farm sound

DOWN

1 Afro-Dominican revolutionary and farmers' rights activist, Mamá ___

2 Perimeter

3 Ruby of *A Raisin in the Sun*

4 Tropical root vegetable

5 Caribbean liquor

42.

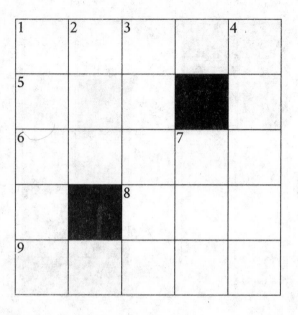

ACROSS

1 Piano or bike part

5 Amount of mics Nas needs

6 State bordering Montana

8 ____ Angeles

9 Small sample of food

DOWN

1 Indicate with a finger

2 Boyz II Men breakup ballad, "____ of the Road"

3 Passes out cards

4 Get ____ (Release your inhibitions, in slang)

7 British comedian Michael Dapaah's viral freestyle, "Man's Not ____"

43.

ACROSS

1 Go against the ___

5 "You've Got Mail" co.

6 Synthetic fabric

7 Brooklyn rapper and entrepreneur, ___-Z

8 Path between buildings

DOWN

1 The Devil's lettuce

2 Meghan Markle, Duchess of Sussex, for example

3 Chemical radical

4 "Bam Bam" singer, Sister ___

44.

ACROSS

1 Very wise person

5 Professor and historian, ____ Louis Gates Jr.

6 Make a case

7 Wall-climbing vines

8 Film spool

DOWN

1 Tennis opening

2 "Wish I Didn't Miss You" singer Stone

3 Bland breakfast

4 "Pretty brown ____, you know I see you / It's a disguise, the way you treat me" (Mint Condition lyrics)

5 Barber shop sweepings

45.

		1	2	3
4	5			
6				
7				
8				

ACROSS

1 *Rap City* channel

4 Ford rival

6 Aged beer

7 "El Negrito Ojos Claros" singer and rapper

8 X, at times

DOWN

1 Already started

2 Divisible by two

3 Banks of fashion

4 Form a clump

5 Jimi Hendrix's "Purple ___"

46.

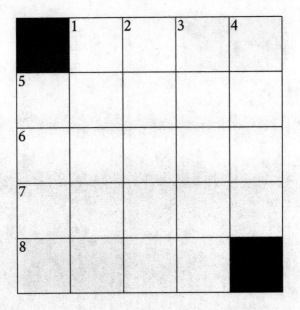

ACROSS

1 What line sisters might do at a pep rally

5 Vortex motion

6 Headwear for 2-DOWN

7 Be a nuisance to

8 Within easy reach

DOWN

1 Pigs and hogs

2 *The Princess and the Frog* protagonist, voiced by Anika Noni Rose

3 Miscalculation

4 *A Raisin in the Sun*, for example

5 Superfan

47.

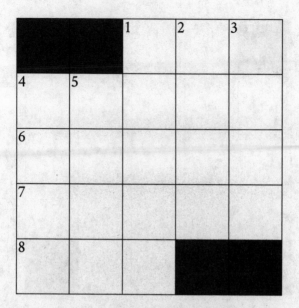

ACROSS

1 Burnable items

4 Steph or Ayesha

6 Vegetable that'll make you cry

7 One half of UGK

8 "Who's That Girl?" rapper

DOWN

1 Felony, e.g.

2 A ____ in the bucket

3 Harmonize

4 Handle adversity

5 Inst. of learning

48.

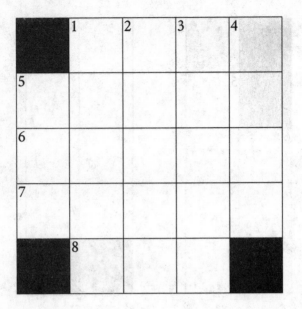

ACROSS

1 All wrapped up

5 1988 Olympic track star, familiarly

6 Hair area that may be tended to with a toothbrush

7 Low card in a deck

8 After-tax amount

DOWN

1 ____ days (long ago)

2 Donyale Luna was the first Black supermodel to cover the British edition of this magazine

3 Remove from a computer

4 1994 Seal hit, "Kiss From a ____"

5 Gave sustenance to

54

49.

	1	2	3	4
■	5			
6				
7				
8				■

ACROSS

1 Org. of Kwame Ture (a.k.a. Stokely Carmichael)

5 Response to "Marco!"

6 "Paid in Full" rapper

7 "___ is on the cut, and my name is [6-ACROSS]"

8 Hit one's highest point

DOWN

1 Fifth tire

2 Cell phone brand

3 Get along well, informally

4 Hot ___ (hairstyling tool)

6 Ayanna Pressley or Cori Bush, e.g.

50.

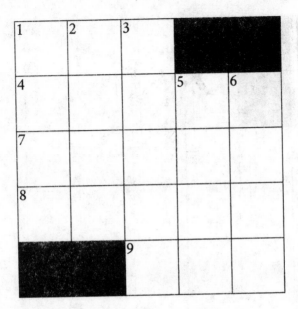

ACROSS

1 Temple University mascot
4 Whoopi's Oscar film
7 *Reading Rainbow* host Burton
8 Colonic treatment
9 1996 hit from Beenie Man and Mya, "Girls ___ Sugar"

DOWN

1 Watch inappropriately
2 A question of timing
3 Cherished
5 ___ time next week?
6 Trolley car

51.

ACROSS

1 Supervillain's HQ

5 In need of a massage

6 Philadelphia NFLer

7 The Divine Nine

8 "You ____ Live Once"

DOWN

1 Boogie Down Productions song championing Black history, "You Must ____"

2 Divine guardian

3 "Choosey Lover" group, The ____ Brothers

4 Smell awful

5 "Pa' Que Retozen" reggaeton innovator Calderón

57

52.

ACROSS

1 Website help section
4 Spelman grad
6 Sha'Carri Richardson's talent
8 Word before park or song
9 Without an ID

DOWN

1 Observe Ramadan, say
2 1906 fraternity, for short
3 "Quiero Bailar" reggaeton legend, Ivy ___
5 Staff note
7 Family room

53.

ACROSS

1 Fuel from a mine
5 Clever ploy
6 "Ting-A-Ling" singer Shabba
7 Formerly
8 Dandelion, for one

DOWN

1 Solange might not be pleased to see one in the sky
2 Two tablespoons
3 Made an inquiry
4 French music duo, ____ Nubians
6 Participate in crew

54.

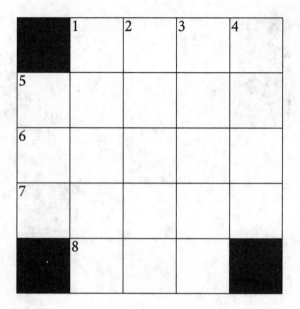

ACROSS

1 "To Be Young, Gifted and Black" singer Simone
5 Meteorological tool
6 Botanical spike
7 Intends (to)
8 Leader of the Family Stone

DOWN

1 Gives a title to
2 Best imaginable
3 18th-century leader of the Jamaican Maroons, Queen ____
4 Performing ____
5 Aries symbol

55.

¹	²	³	▓	▓
⁴			⁵	⁶
⁷				
⁸				
⁹				

ACROSS

1 2004 Denzel Washington thriller, ____ *on Fire*

4 Afro-Dominican musician and reality star, ____ La Negra

7 "Ain't no mountain high enough / Ain't no valley low enough / Ain't no ____ wide enough / To keep me from getting to you, babe"

8 Iconic 1993 song from the Wu-Tang Clan

9 Like rolling terrain

DOWN

1 1997 demonstration in Philadelphia, Million Woman ____

2 Poet Baraka

3 Belly button

5 Not phony

6 Military group

56.

1		2	3	4
		5		
6	7			
8				
9				

ACROSS

1 Used a beeper

5 Messenger strands

6 Straighten, as car wheels

8 Bunk

9 Sled dog breed

DOWN

1 Type of cobbler

2 Shrimp and ___

3 H.S. subject

4 *Lethal Weapon* actor Glover

7 "You'll Never Find Another Love Like Mine" singer Rawls

57.

	1	2	3	4
	5			
6				
7				
8				

ACROSS

1 Champagne glass part

5 "Day 'N' Nite" musician, Kid ____

6 Dwellings

7 Hotel offerings

8 Hose output

DOWN

1 Timbaland & Magoo collaborator, Fatman ____

2 Abnormal cell growth

3 Fluid buildup

4 Hip-hop artist, ____ "Misdemeanor" Elliott

6 60-min. periods

58.

	1	2	3	4
5				
6				
7				
8				

ACROSS

1 It's right on the map

5 A style of Jamaican folk music, predating ska and reggae

6 Instrument with pipes

7 Alabama rapper, Flo ___

8 Search for

DOWN

1 Like a haunted house

2 It may be acute, right, or obtuse

3 Piece of celery

4 "You're Makin' Me High" singer Braxton

5 They're honored in May

59.

1	2	3	4	5
6				
7				
8			■	
9				

ACROSS

1 ____ it on the alcohol
6 Permissible by law
7 Formally revise
8 Puerto Rican reggaeton star Omar
9 Big key on a computer keyboard

DOWN

1 Razor or knife
2 Water garnish
3 Contract negotiator
4 "I'm starting with the ____ in the mirror / I'm asking him to change his ways"
5 Tribal leader, often

65

60.

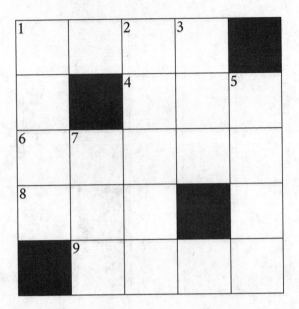

ACROSS

1 Unhinged, in Spanish
4 Limb with biceps and triceps
6 Cuban musical genre and dance
8 "Girl, ___"
9 Tweet hit "___ (Oh My)"

DOWN

1 Young sheep
2 "Word Up!" band
3 Celestial sphere
5 Green growth
7 Actress Edebiri of *The Bear* and *Bottoms*

61.

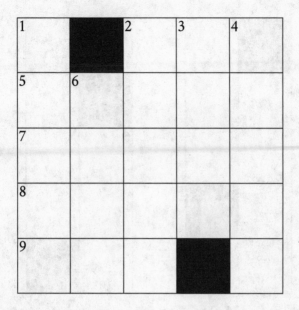

ACROSS

2 End of many co. names

5 Propose

7 New Hampshire neighbor

8 Stacks

9 Entirely

DOWN

1 Haiti's national music

2 PBS news anchor Gwen

3 "I said what I said" reality star Leakes

4 Top of a wave

6 Be unsuccessful

62.

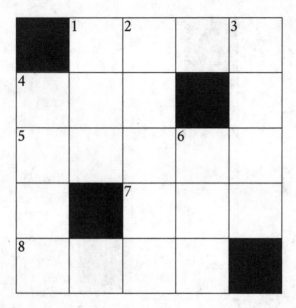

ACROSS

1 One who's joined the cause
4 "In Ha Mood" rapper, ____ Spice
5 "Life for me ain't been no crystal ____" (Line from Langston Hughes' "Mother to Son")
7 Damon Wayans Jr. to Damon Wayans
8 Church affirmation

DOWN

1 What Regina King can do really well
2 Rental agreement
3 Knitting material
4 Hollywood tycoon Rae
6 + or – particle

63.

ACROSS

1 ____ acres and a mule
5 Actor Epps of 1992 film *Juice*
6 Defiant type
8 *Suits* actress Torres
9 Pops

DOWN

1 In favor of
2 ____ Psi Phi Fraternity
3 Foaming at the mouth
4 Current fashion
7 Deposit eggs

64.

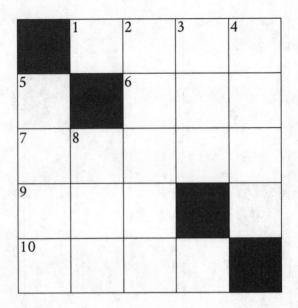

ACROSS

1 Made better with time
6 Bourbon cousin
7 Stainless ____
9 Go number one
10 A level of vocal ability above "sing"

DOWN

2 Annual guidebook for African American travelers during the Jim Crow era, *The Negro Motorist* ____ *Book*
3 Toni Morrison's *The Bluest* ____
4 PC brand
5 Priority Mail org.
8 Matcha, e.g.

65.

ACROSS

1 1965 Los Angeles uprising, the ____ Rebellion
5 Enjoy Thanksgiving
6 Afro–Puerto Rican traditional musical style and dance
8 Once ____ a time
9 Offered one's seat

DOWN

1 Spider's craft
2 Musical pace
3 Socially unacceptable
4 Ben E. King's "____ By Me"
7 Not at home

66.

	1	2	3	4
5				
6				
7				
8				

ACROSS

1 Melanin-deficient in the winter, say

5 Had the nerve

6 Overthrow

7 *How to Be an Antiracist* author Ibram X.

8 Clear the board

DOWN

1 Money, in slang

2 Concert venue

3 Gives temporarily

4 Murphy of *Coming to America*

5 Ellington of jazz

67.

ACROSS

1 Book ID

5 *Living Single* character Maxine

6 2020 US Open winner Naomi

7 *Food & Liquor* rapper Fiasco

8 Road sign animal

DOWN

1 Magazine edition

2 Give form to

3 Civil rights activist Ella

4 *Straight Outta Compton* group

6 Antique

68.

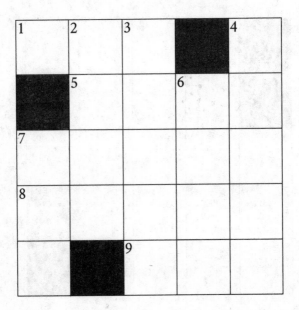

ACROSS

1 SUV maker

5 Furthermore

7 Hiker's route

8 The first independent Black country in the "New World"

9 1975 poetry book by Nikki Giovanni, *The Women and the* ____

DOWN

2 *Girlfriends* creator, ____ Brock Akil

3 Assert

4 Quarterback and civil rights activist Kaepernick

6 Web location

7 However, informally

69.

ACROSS

1 Houston rapper, ____ Thee Stallion

5 Ransack

6 Barber's sharpener

8 Idris of *The Wire*

9 Earliest stage

DOWN

1 Bride's title, perhaps

2 "Have you ____ today?"

3 Miami rap duo, City ____

4 Photoshop company

7 Makeup artist and entrepreneur McGrath

70.

ACROSS

1 Tennis great Williams
5 Center of rotation
6 From dusk to dawn
8 Look rudely
9 *Scandal* actress Washington

DOWN

1 Moving day vehicle
2 Kick out of the country
3 Nation north of Benin
4 "Confessions" R&B singer
7 "If at first you don't succeed / Then dust yourself off and ___ again" (Aaliyah lyrics)

71.

ACROSS

1 "You ____ that!" (Great job!)
4 Name on a title
6 The Cha Cha Slide, for example
7 It may be existential
8 Cook in a pan

DOWN

1 Sort of star
2 "____ City Blues" (Marvin Gaye song)
3 Deteriorate
4 Hip-hop music collective, ____ Future
5 Wine choice

72.

¹	²	³	⁴	■
⁵				■
⁶				⁷
⁸				
■	⁹			

ACROSS

1 Unlikely, as chances
5 Horne or Waithe
6 In the loop
8 Gold digger
9 Spotted

DOWN

1 Poetry ___
2 Civil rights icon John
3 Absurd
4 *Emergent Strategy* author, adrienne ___ brown
7 Shore bird

73.

ACROSS

1 2005 drama starring Terrence Howard and Taraji P. Henson, *Hustle & ____*
5 Michigan or Ontario
6 Sets of twins
7 Dazzling effect
8 First Black sorority, for short

DOWN

1 "Killing Me Softly with His Song" singer Roberta
2 Undefeated Ali
3 Cajun veggie
4 Toward the setting sun
6 Split ____ soup

74.

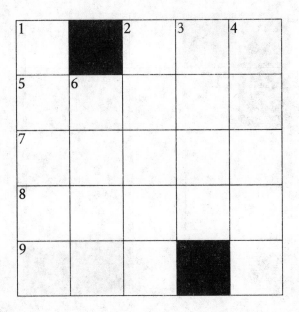

ACROSS

2 A pair

5 Survey question option

7 Far-reaching

8 "Me Too" movement founder Tarana

9 Japanese money

DOWN

1 "My Prerogative" singer Brown

2 Rose hazard

3 Too diluted

4 It's placed in a restaurant

6 ___ that ("I agree")

75.

1	■	2	3	4
5	6			
7				
8				
9			■	

ACROSS

2 Prefix with information

5 Love dearly

7 Oscar winner Cicely

8 Most high school students

9 Org. you send taxes to

DOWN

1 "If Only You Knew" singer LaBelle

2 "Be Your Girl (Kaytranada Edition)" singer Teedra

3 Cast ___ skillet

4 Gut feeling

6 Fabric colorer

76.

ACROSS

1 2020 album from Nigerian singer Wizkid, *Made in* ___

5 www address

6 Viola da ___

8 Sacred bird in Ancient Egypt

9 Soup base

DOWN

1 Drumstick

2 Creole stew

3 Planetary path

4 Cut, as prices

7 ___ Jordan sneakers

77.

1	2	3		
4			5	6
7				
8				
		9		

ACROSS

1 DJ EZ Rock counterpart, ____ Base

4 Put up, as a monument

7 Oscar winner Berry

8 NBA Hall of Famer Iverson

9 Poetic "over there"

DOWN

1 Detox facility

2 Like some hygiene

3 1998 crime drama by director Hype Williams

5 TV psychic, Miss ____

6 Fisk Univ state

78.

ACROSS

2 Young fellow
5 Sheep-related
7 Going to, in Southern slang
8 Found the sum
9 Red and White, in baseball

DOWN

1 Living room fixture
2 *Da 5 Bloods* actor, Delroy ____
3 Building addition
4 Wrong or presidents
6 YouTube content, for short

79.

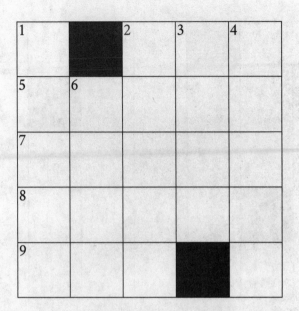

ACROSS

2 Summer in California, on a clock

5 Falcon's nest

7 Lupita Nyong'o played one in *Star Wars: The Force Awakens*

8 2002 love song by Common and Mary J. Blige, "Come ___"

9 ___ for the course

DOWN

1 Civil rights org. with Image Awards

2 At an earlier time

3 Runs out of juice

4 Core principle

6 Jazz legend Fitzgerald

80.

ACROSS

1 Browsing history
5 "You can't turn me ____ / You better believe in your heart I always want to stay"
6 Barry of baseball
8 *A Subtlety* artist Walker
9 Calm down

DOWN

1 Vehicle with a meter
2 Heard the alarm clock
3 Panama passage
4 Many-headed water monster
7 Kamasi Washington's instrument

81.

ACROSS

1 Pop singer Derulo
5 Common flooring wood
6 "___ done, hair done, everything did"
8 Place to park
9 Goofy

DOWN

1 Who? Mike ____
2 Letters on little batteries
3 Proficiency
4 "My first name ain't baby, it's Janet / Miss Jackson if you're ___"
7 Texter's chuckle

82.

ACROSS

1 Count of jazz
5 Australian avian
6 Twisting the truth
8 Low digit
9 "It's mine, I ____ it"

DOWN

1 Hits a powerful high note
2 Painter Sherald
3 *Maxwell's Urban Hang* ____
4 Trimmed, as a lawn
7 ____-binary

83.

1	2	3	4	
5				■
6				7
■	8			
9				

ACROSS

1 Tightly packed

5 Coveted award status Viola Davis and Quincy Jones have in common, Abbr.

6 Cast a ballot

8 Fashion model Marcille

9 Filled with cargo

DOWN

1 2021 Hanif Abdurraqib book, *A Little ____ in America*

2 2015 album by The Internet, ____ *Death*

3 Wrote down

4 *Family Feud* host Harvey

7 Harlem fashion designer, Dapper ____

89

84.

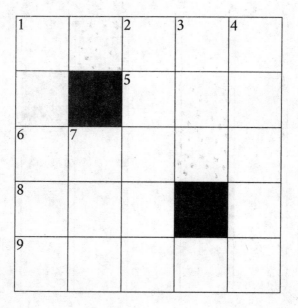

ACROSS

1 Capricorn and Aquarius
5 ___-DMC
6 Fuming
8 Lobbying letters
9 It might be ordered well-done

DOWN

1 Sends by USPS, say
2 Jones or Wales Bonner
3 Pistachio or pecan
4 ___ diss
7 Snitch

85.

¹		²	³	⁴
■	■	⁵		
⁶	⁷			
⁸			■	■
⁹				

ACROSS

1 Actor, singer, and comic Foxx

5 Flattering poem

6 "Kissin' You" R&B group

8 Turnt

9 Notice or uncover something, in slang

DOWN

2 YOLO, for one

3 Civil rights leader, ____ B. Wells

4 Slippery, long fish

6 *CrazySexyCool* group

7 Castor or jojoba

86.

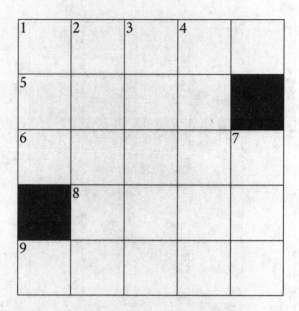

ACROSS

1 Units of land area

5 Will's uncle in *The Fresh Prince of Bel-Air*

6 House overhangs

8 "Otro Trago" singer from Panama

9 Dr. Shabazz

DOWN

1 Chimp or gorilla

2 Run after

3 Heavy metal fastener

4 Put into political power

7 Not outgoing

87.

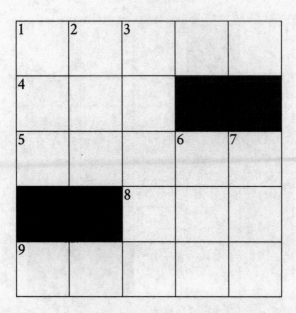

ACROSS

1 Philadelphia rapper Tierra

4 *Abbott Elementary* channel

5 Point guard Trae

8 Cause for overtime

9 Lacking competence

DOWN

1 Path or route

2 *Random Acts of Flyness* network

3 Under 90 degrees

6 Puppy's bite

7 "___ Up Offa That Thing"

88.

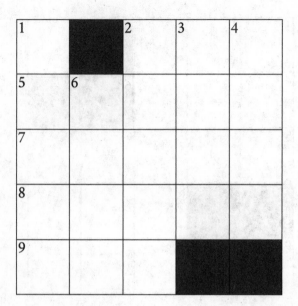

ACROSS

2 Low-lit
5 Make very happy
7 Activist Angela
8 Out of place
9 Showed the way

DOWN

1 Olympic prize
2 Baseball's "Big Papi" Ortiz
3 Sleepy feeling after consuming too much food
4 A hot ____
6 Poor, as an excuse

89.

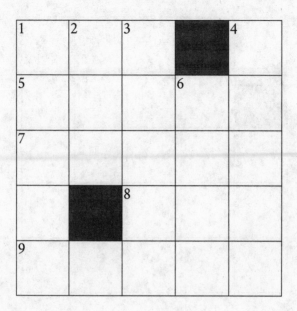

ACROSS

1 Mac alternatives

5 Pulitzer-winning musician Kendrick

7 Licorice flavored seed

8 "____ Boy Is Mine"

9 Had throbbing pain

DOWN

1 Shopping complex

2 "Sunny days, everybody loves them, tell me, baby / ____ you stand the rain?"

3 *White Teeth* novelist Zadie

4 Dog classification

6 1975 Wimbledon winner Arthur

90.

1	2	3	4	5
■	6			
7				
8			■	
9				

ACROSS

1 Rosa or Gordon

6 1982 Dazz Band hit, "Let It ____"

7 Brady of *Whose Line Is It Anyway?*

8 Popular msg. service in the '90s and '00s

9 Cardiologist's insert

DOWN

2 Stand by for

3 What rappers do

4 Your relatives

5 Went through the letters of

7 What had happened ____

91.

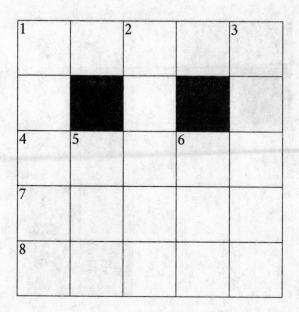

ACROSS

1 Motown legend Ross
4 Adjust to a situation
7 Racket
8 "Bossy" singer and farmer

DOWN

1 Got hydrated
2 To no ____
3 Chips before deals
5 Anonymous Jane
6 Kappa Alpha ____ fraternity

92.

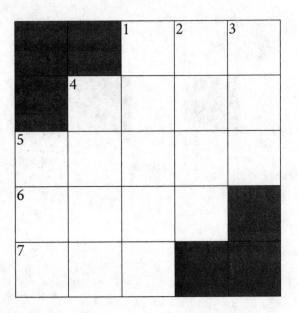

ACROSS

1 First person to "cross" in a Greek organization line
4 Admired celebrity
5 Frenzied way to run
6 Savory Haitian stew made with jute leaves and spinach
7 Congestion doc

DOWN

1 Young ___ fiction
2 2023 US Open winner Gauff
3 Animal with antlers
4 Somali-American model and actress known mononymously
5 Beer relative

93.

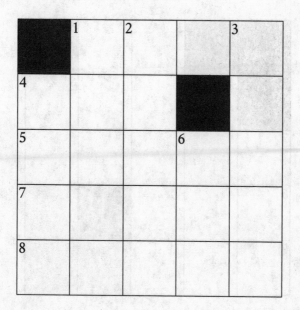

ACROSS

1 Airport boarding site
4 Cookie container
5 Eagle's nest
7 "Come ____ and ride on a fantastic voyage"
8 Full of current events

DOWN

1 Morning TV personality King
2 ONE WAY sign shape
3 Somber poem
4 Neo-expressionist artist, ____-Michel Basquiat
6 Stand-____ (subs)

94.

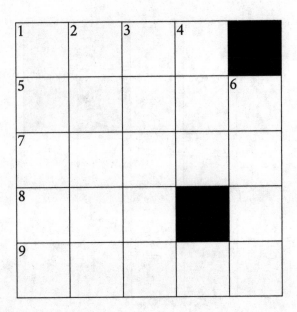

ACROSS

1 Afro-Dominican singer Valoy

5 Selfish types

7 What your skin might do if you add an exfoliant to your routine

8 Furious feeling

9 Sociology professor and author, Michael Eric ___

DOWN

1 A song by 112 you might play on Valentine's Day

2 Exorbitant interest

3 Dwarf planet between Mars and Jupiter

4 Charity's URL ender

6 "Get Busy" musician Paul

95.

ACROSS

1 TV monitoring group, Abbr.

4 It's a ____ (it's over, in slang)

6 Hair protector and wave preserver

8 Insignificant

9 Unit of computer memory

DOWN

1 NBA position, Abbr.

2 Bread remnant

3 "Queen of Christmas" Mariah

5 Split

7 Exclamation that sounds like a letter

96.

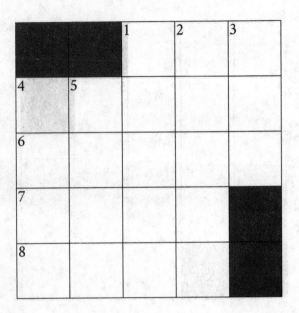

ACROSS

1 Score units, briefly
4 Hang down
6 April forecast
7 Salicylic acid target
8 Understands

DOWN

1 On ___ (Very impressive, in slang)
2 Hues
3 Josephine Baker during WWII
4 With 5-DOWN, RuPaul's reality competition
5 See 4-DOWN

97.

ACROSS

1 "I know, I know, yep, yeah, you ____ / Okay, everybody meet Mr. Me ____" (Clipse lyrics)

4 Release, as energy

6 *Kind of Blue* trumpeter Davis

8 Prepare, as tea

9 Genetic letters

DOWN

1 Nigerian "Free Mind" singer

2 Exclude from the list

3 Like a moisturized scalp

5 New driver, typically

7 Place to get a facial

98.

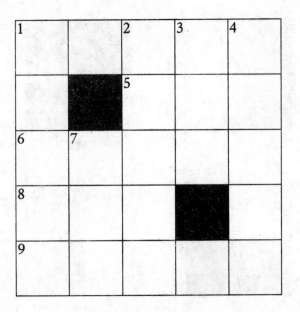

ACROSS

1 2.2-pound measures, for short

5 Sister Sledge hit, "We ___ Family"

6 Challenged on foot

8 Poor People's Campaign monogram

9 Supermarket section

DOWN

1 Cosmic consequences

2 *The Immortal Life of Henrietta* ___

3 Mine extraction

4 Wetlands growth

7 Actor Mahershala of *True Detective*

99.

ACROSS

1 Fuel efficiency no
4 Heavenly Gospel Singers' "Take My Hand, Precious ____"
6 Jumping the ____
8 CP ____
9 Previously unreleased

DOWN

1 Org. Roberto Clemente played in for eighteen seasons
2 Place to dock
3 It can be pulled while running
5 Top of a mosque
7 Kitten's cry

100.

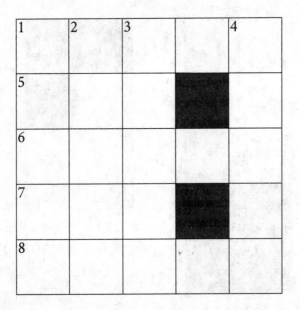

ACROSS

1 A guy that can't get no love from TLC

5 Opposite of post-

6 Itching to go

7 *13th* director DuVernay

8 Rowland of Destiny's Child

DOWN

1 "When we are silent, we are still afraid, so it is better to ___." —Audre Lorde

2 Have an urge for

3 Majestic

4 *Moonlight* director Jenkins

ANSWERS

1.

S	A	M		
A	L	I	A	S
D	I	S	C	O
	C	T	R	L
	E	Y	E	D

2.

F	A	L	L	
A	L	L	O	W
S	T	A	G	E
T	A	M	I	A
	R	A	C	K

3.

J	E	T		
A	N	I	T	A
M	A	G	I	C
	T	E	N	T
	E	R	A	S

4.

B	U	D		
A	S	I	A	N
S	A	L	S	A
S	I	L	K	Y
	N	A	S	

5.

M	B	A		
A	R	I	S	E
T	I	L	E	S
S	C	E	N	T
	K	Y	D	

6.

	H	A	R	D
D	O	N	O	R
U	N	D	U	E
S	O	R	T	S
T	R	E	E	S

7.

C	O	S	T	
O	P	T	I	C
A	R	O	M	A
S	A	V	E	S
T	H	E	R	E

8.

T	H	I	N	
R	O	S	E	
I	M	A	G	E
P	E	A	R	L
		C	A	M

9.

S	U	P		
T	P	A	I	N
A	S	I	D	E
R	E	N	E	W
E	T	T	A	

10.

	R	A	P	
M	O	V	E	D
A	B	A	T	E
L	I	N	E	N
E	N	T	R	Y

11.

	S	M	S	
H	O	O	K	S
A	N	N	I	E
S	I	G	M	A
	C	O	P	

12.

	D	U	B	
P	I	L	O	T
I	N	T	R	O
C	A	R	E	T
S	H	A	D	E

13.

P	R	A	Y	
R	U	L	E	R
O	P	E	R	A
P	E	R	R	Y
S	E	T		

14.

A	D	O	P	T
S	O	N	I	A
S	N	E	E	R
E	N	A	C	T
T	A	L	E	

15.

	S	A	L	T
R	O	D	E	O
H	U	M	A	N
O	L	I	V	E
A	S	T	E	R

16.

	W	E	E	P
W	I	L	L	I
A	L	I	V	E
D	E	T	E	R
E	Y	E	S	

111

17.

M	A	T		
A	D	A	M	S
C	I	L	I	A
E	N	E	M	Y
O	A	S	I	S

18.

F	L	A	S	H
R	E	V		O
I	T	E	M	S
E		N	A	T
D	I	S	C	S

19.

		R	O	M
	S	O	C	A
L	A	M	E	S
I	D	E	A	S
L	E	O	N	

20.

K	I	S	S	
I	D	L	E	R
T	R	A	D	E
T	I	T	A	N
	S	E	N	T

21.

		J	A	B
	C	U	T	E
B	A	I	L	E
O	S	C	A	R
P	A	Y	S	

22.

T		S	A	C
U	S	U	A	L
L	E	A	V	E
S	A	V	E	R
A	T	E		K

23.

R	I	S	K	
A	N	T	I	
S	T	E	E	R
T	E	A	S	E
A	R	M	E	D

24.

F	D	A		
L	E	N	N	Y
A	L	G	A	E
S	L	E	P	T
K	A	L	E	

25.

	S	P	A	T
D	O	L	C	E
A	W	A	K	E
F	E	T	E	
T	R	E	E	

26.

	C	U	S	P
B	A	N	T	U
O	R	I	O	N
A	G	O	N	Y
T	O	N	E	

27.

M	A	C		
A	D	A	G	E
N	O	S	E	D
G	R	I	O	T
U	N	O		

28.

	S	U	R	F
B	A	N	A	L
U	N	I	T	E
L	A	T	E	X
B	A	Y	S	

114

29.

K	I	M		
I	C	E	T	
T	I	D	A	L
	N	I	C	E
	G	A	T	E

30.

S	C	O	T	T
P		W	A	R
A	L	I	B	I
W	I	N		N
N	E	G	G	A

31.

	B	H	M	
A	L	O	O	F
R	O	N	D	O
C	O	D	E	X
	D	A	M	

32.

S	T	A	T	E
M	A	R	I	A
A	M	B	E	R
S	P	O	R	T
H	A	R	S	H

115

33.

	T	R	A	P
P	R	O	M	O
R	O	S	E	S
O	P	I	N	E
S	E	E	D	

34.

L	A	R	C	H
O	M	A	H	A
C	I	V	I	L
K	N	E	L	L
S	E	N	D	

35.

		B	U	S
A	B	U	S	E
B	E	R	E	T
L	A	N	D	S
E	R	A		

36.

C	A	S	E	S
O	B	A	M	A
V	O	W	E	L
E	V	E	N	T
T	E	D	D	Y

37.

S	H	I	N	
L	I	S	A	
A	L	L	O	Y
B	L	A	M	E
		M	I	A

38.

C	A	M		
A	B	A	S	H
P	L	U	T	O
	O	V	A	L
	H	E	R	E

39.

	G	E	M	
R	E	L	A	Y
I	N	D	Y	A
C	R	E	A	M
H	E	R		

40.

A	B	S		
R	I	C	E	
A	L	A	R	M
B	E	L	I	E
	S	E	C	T

41.

		T	E	D
	T	I	D	E
R	A	N	G	E
U	R	G	E	
M	O	O		

42.

P	E	D	A	L
O	N	E		O
I	D	A	H	O
N		L	O	S
T	A	S	T	E

43.

G	R	A	I	N
A	O	L		A
N	Y	L	O	N
J	A	Y		C
A	L	L	E	Y

44.

	S	A	G	E
H	E	N	R	Y
A	R	G	U	E
I	V	I	E	S
R	E	E	L	

45.

		B	E	T
C	H	E	V	Y
L	A	G	E	R
O	Z	U	N	A
T	E	N		

46.

	S	T	E	P
S	W	I	R	L
T	I	A	R	A
A	N	N	O	Y
N	E	A	R	

47.

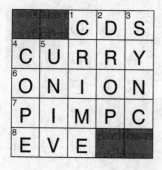

		C	D	S
C	U	R	R	Y
O	N	I	O	N
P	I	M	P	C
E	V	E		

48.

	O	V	E	R
F	L	O	J	O
E	D	G	E	S
D	E	U	C	E
	N	E	T	

49.

	S	N	C	C
	P	O	L	O
R	A	K	I	M
E	R	I	C	B
P	E	A	K	

50.

O	W	L		
G	H	O	S	T
L	E	V	A	R
E	N	E	M	A
		D	E	M

51.

	L	A	I	R
T	E	N	S	E
E	A	G	L	E
G	R	E	E	K
O	N	L	Y	

52.

F	A	Q		
A	L	U	M	
S	P	E	E	D
T	H	E	M	E
	A	N	O	N

53.

	C	O	A	L
	R	U	S	E
R	A	N	K	S
O	N	C	E	
W	E	E	D	

54.

	N	I	N	A
R	A	D	A	R
A	M	E	N	T
M	E	A	N	S
	S	L	Y	

55.

M	A	N		
A	M	A	R	A
R	I	V	E	R
C	R	E	A	M
H	I	L	L	Y

56.

P	A	G	E	D
E		R	N	A
A	L	I	G	N
C	O	T		N
H	U	S	K	Y

57.

	S	T	E	M
	C	U	D	I
H	O	M	E	S
R	O	O	M	S
S	P	R	A	Y

58.

	E	A	S	T
M	E	N	T	O
O	R	G	A	N
M	I	L	L	I
S	E	E	K	

59.

B	L	A	M	E
L	E	G	A	L
A	M	E	N	D
D	O	N		E
E	N	T	E	R

60.

L	O	C	O	
A		A	R	M
M	A	M	B	O
B	Y	E		S
	O	O	P	S

122

61.

¹K		²I	³N	⁴C
⁵O	⁶F	F	E	R
⁷M	A	I	N	E
⁸P	I	L	E	S
⁹A	L	L		T

62.

	¹A	²L	L	³Y
⁴I	C	E		A
⁵S	T	A	⁶I	R
S		⁷S	O	N
⁸A	M	E	N	

63.

¹F	²O	³R	⁴T	Y
⁵O	M	A	R	
⁶R	E	B	E	⁷L
	⁸G	I	N	A
⁹D	A	D	D	Y

64.

	¹A	²G	³E	⁴D
⁵U		⁶R	Y	E
⁷S	⁸T	E	E	L
⁹P	E	E		L
¹⁰S	A	N	G	

65.

W	A	T	T	S
E		E	A	T
B	O	M	B	A
	U	P	O	N
S	T	O	O	D

66.

	P	A	L	E
D	A	R	E	D
U	P	E	N	D
K	E	N	D	I
E	R	A	S	E

67.

	I	S	B	N
	S	H	A	W
O	S	A	K	A
L	U	P	E	
D	E	E	R	

68.

G	M	C		C
	A	L	S	O
T	R	A	I	L
H	A	I	T	I
O		M	E	N

69.

M	E	G	A	N
R	A	I	D	■
S	T	R	O	P
■	E	L	B	A
O	N	S	E	T

70.

V	E	N	U	S
A	X	I	S	■
N	I	G	H	T
■	L	E	E	R
K	E	R	R	Y

71.

■	D	I	D	■
O	W	N	E	R
D	A	N	C	E
D	R	E	A	D
■	F	R	Y	■

72.

S	L	I	M	■
L	E	N	A	■
A	W	A	R	E
M	I	N	E	R
■	S	E	E	N

73.

	F	L	O	W
	L	A	K	E
P	A	I	R	S
E	C	L	A	T
A	K	A		

74.

B		T	W	O
O	T	H	E	R
B	R	O	A	D
B	U	R	K	E
Y	E	N		R

75.

P		M	I	S
A	D	O	R	E
T	Y	S	O	N
T	E	E	N	S
I	R	S		E

76.

L	A	G	O	S
E		U	R	L
G	A	M	B	A
	I	B	I	S
B	R	O	T	H

77.

R	O	B		
E	R	E	C	T
H	A	L	L	E
A	L	L	E	N
B		Y	O	N

78.

S		L	A	D
O	V	I	N	E
F	I	N	N	A
A	D	D	E	D
	S	O	X	

79.

N		P	D	T
A	E	R	I	E
A	L	I	E	N
C	L	O	S	E
P	A	R		T

80.

C	A	C	H	E
A	W	A	Y	
B	O	N	D	S
	K	A	R	A
R	E	L	A	X

127

81.

J	A	S	O	N
O	A	K	■	A
N	A	I	L	S
E	■	L	O	T
S	I	L	L	Y

82.

B	A	S	I	E
E	M	U	■	D
L	Y	I	N	G
T	■	T	O	E
S	P	E	N	D

83.

D	E	N	S	E
E	G	O	T	■
V	O	T	E	D
I	■	E	V	A
L	A	D	E	N

84.

S	I	G	N	S
H	■	R	U	N
I	R	A	T	E
P	A	C	■	A
S	T	E	A	K

128

85.

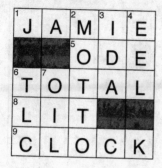

J	A	M	I	E
		O	D	E
T	O	T	A	L
L	I	T		
C	L	O	C	K

86.

A	C	R	E	S
P	H	I	L	
E	A	V	E	S
	S	E	C	H
B	E	T	T	Y

87.

W	H	A	C	K
A	B	C		
Y	O	U	N	G
		T	I	E
I	N	E	P	T

88.

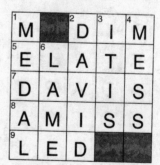

M		D	I	M
E	L	A	T	E
D	A	V	I	S
A	M	I	S	S
L	E	D		

89.

P	C	S	■	B
L	A	M	A	R
A	N	I	S	E
Z	■	T	H	E
A	C	H	E	D

90.

P	A	R	K	S
■	W	H	I	P
W	A	Y	N	E
A	I	M	■	L
S	T	E	N	T

91.

D	I	A	N	A
R	■	V	■	N
A	D	A	P	T
N	O	I	S	E
K	E	L	I	S

92.

■	■	A	C	E
■	I	D	O	L
A	M	U	C	K
L	A	L	O	■
E	N	T	■	■

93.

	G	A	T	E
J	A	R		L
E	Y	R	I	E
A	L	O	N	G
N	E	W	S	Y

94.

C	U	C	O	
U	S	E	R	S
P	U	R	G	E
I	R	E		A
D	Y	S	O	N

95.

F	C	C		
W	R	A	P	
D	U	R	A	G
	M	E	R	E
	B	Y	T	E

96.

		P	T	S
D	R	O	O	P
R	A	I	N	Y
A	C	N	E	
G	E	T	S	

131

97.

¹T	O	³O		
⁴E	M	I	T	
⁶M	I	L	E	⁷S
⁸S	T	E	E	P
		⁹D	N	A

98.

¹K	I	²L	³O	⁴S
A		⁵A	R	E
⁶R	⁷A	C	E	D
⁸M	L	K		G
⁹A	I	S	L	E

99.

¹M	P	³G		
⁴L	O	R	⁵D	
⁶B	R	O	O	⁷M
	⁸T	I	M	E
		⁹N	E	W

100.

¹S	C	³R	U	⁴B
⁵P	R	E		A
⁶E	A	G	E	R
⁷A	V	A		R
⁸K	E	L	L	Y

132

ACKNOWLEDGMENTS

I'd first like to thank all the passionate supporters and solvers of Black Crossword, who made such a splash upon our launch in January 2023 that this book was made possible in a relatively short amount of time. When I first had the idea to start this, I thought it was something I would like to play, and I'm so ecstatic to be a witness to the joy the puzzles bring to others.

To the "Crossworld," thank you all for being so curious and creative, and incredibly supportive of Black Crossword. I had no idea just how deep this community is, and it has been a true delight to be a part of it.

Huge thank-yous to Patrik Bass and Daphney Guillaume for thoughtfully editing and guiding this book, and for being so patient with my many, many questions. I'm so grateful for you both and feel so lucky to have had your input.

To the entire team at Amistad and HarperCollins, thank you for believing in this book, for seeing its purpose, and for betting on its potential.

ACKNOWLEDGMENTS

To Kristian Brown, I am so appreciative of your guidance and your brilliance. You are remarkable at what you do.

Thank you Angeline Rodriguez and everyone at WME for making this book happen with patience and intention.

I'm endlessly indebted to the work of Black historians across the diaspora.

To my community of loved ones—I am incredibly blessed to share time and space with you. Thank you.

ABOUT THE AUTHOR

JULIANA PACHE is the founder of Black Crossword. After obtaining her BA in media studies from Temple University, she worked as a social and digital marketing professional at various brands and publications such as Red Bull, the *Fader*, *Vice*, and *Rolling Stone*. When she's not working on Black Crossword, she creates handmade jewelry for her online shop, Pache Studio. She lives in Brooklyn.

julianapache.com | @thecityofjules
blackcrossword.com | @blackcrossword